# Women of the Celts